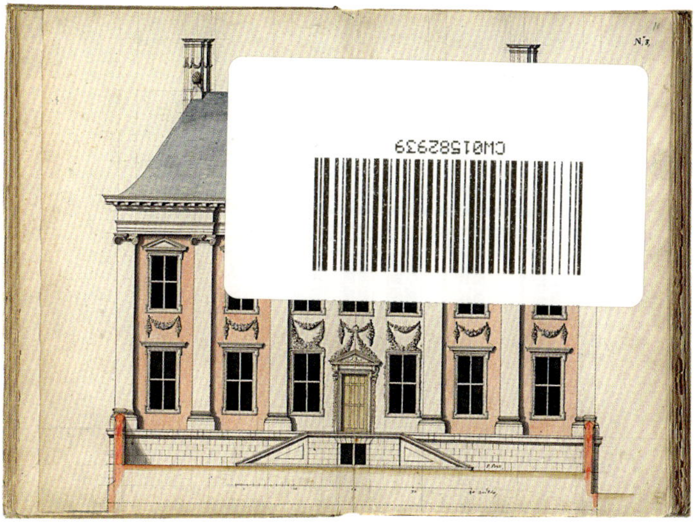

Pieter Post
Haarlem 1608–1669, The Hague
Facade of the Mauritshuis, 1652
Pen and ink on paper, 41.9 × 53.5 cm
National Library of the Netherlands, The Hague

responsible for making the House of Orange's collection of paintings princely again in the eighteenth century. In 1774 William V constructed a picture gallery for the collection, which was accessible to the public. This was the first public art collection in Holland – a milestone in Dutch museum history. (The Prince William V Gallery, which was reopened in 2010 after renovation work, now falls under the aegis of the Mauritshuis.) When Napoleon invaded Holland in 1795, William V's collection was seized and taken to the Louvre in Paris. After Napoleon's defeat at the Battle of Waterloo, the paintings were returned to the Netherlands, and King William I sold the entire collection to the state in 1816.

The Mauritshuis has recently undertaken an ambitious plan to renovate and expand the museum. To mark the occasion, I have written this book, which offers a personal selection of highlights from the collection. These include a work that hangs in the Prince William V Gallery (see pp.20–1), recent acquisitions (see pp.28–9, 40–1) and some of my favourites. They are arranged roughly in chronological order and by genre. The comments are highly personal and any errors are my own. I hope that you will have as much pleasure in reading this book as I have had in writing it, and that you will have the opportunity to see the paintings included here in the renovated Mauritshuis.

Hans Memling
Seligenstadt *c.*1440–1494 Bruges

Portrait of a Man from the Lespinette Family, *c.*1485–90
Oil on panel, 30.1 × 22.3 cm
Acquired with the support of the Rembrandt Association, 1895
MH 595

This exquisite portrait is what I think of as a typical 'Mauritshuis picture': small in format, in outstanding condition and filled with marvellous details. No wonder one of my predecessors, Abraham Bredius, bid for it keenly at a London auction in July 1894, where the lot was attributed to the Italian painter Antonello da Messina (before 1456–1479). Bredius was convinced that the work was painted by Hans Memling, who was not represented in any public Dutch collection at the time, and went on bidding until he had exceeded the museum's annual acquisitions budget more than twice. Bredius' hunch turned out to have been correct, and this remains the only portrait by Memling in a Dutch museum to this day.

The portrait would originally have been the right half of a diptych, facing a depiction of the Virgin and Child to whom the sitter would have been addressing his prayers. We have been unable to identify the man in this picture, but we know from a coat of arms on the back of the panel that he was from the Lespinette family (also known as De l'Espinette or De Lépinette) from Arlay in Franche-Comté, an area of Burgundy that is now part of France. Memling depicted the man with such refinement that we seem to see every detail of his appearance, from the silky lynx fur of his doublet to the scar on his nose. Memling was the first artist to place sitters in front of a landscape. It is tempting to think that the little church in the left-hand background might have been on the Lespinette estate.

Gerard David
Oudewater *c.*1450–1523 Bruges

Forest Scene, *c.*1505–15
Oil on two panels, each 89.9 × 30.7cm
On long-term loan from the Rijksmuseum, Amsterdam, since 1948
MH 843

As a student of art history, I was taught that these paintings were the first 'pure' landscapes in the history of Northern European art. Our thinking has changed since then – these panels are actually the exterior of a triptych that is now in the collection of the Metropolitan Museum of Art in New York. They were separated from it between 1930 and 1932, because they were believed, erroneously, to be by another hand. When open, the altarpiece showed the Nativity in the central panel and portraits of the donors and Saints Jerome and Leonard on either side. Exterior panels of such a triptych would normally have shown a Biblical scene, such as the Annunciation or Adam and Eve. When this one was closed, all you saw was a lush forest scene, which might possibly have referred to the world as it existed before the coming of the Messiah (Isaiah 32:11–20).

These paintings are small and rather narrow, but David used this format to make the trees tower overhead. The rendering of the leaves is so detailed that we can make out the type of trees (from left to right, an oak, a white walnut and a beech). The only signs of human life are the road and building; the scene is populated by a bird, an ox and two asses. The panels join beautifully, and together they exude the peace of a sleepy summer afternoon.

Hans Holbein the Younger
Augsburg 1497/8–1543 London

***Portrait of Robert Cheseman*, 1533**

Oil on panel, 58.8 × 62.8 cm

Acquired by the Stadholder-King William III, after 1688

MH 276

This remarkable portrait was restored for an exhibition about Holbein held at the Mauritshuis in 2003. The show was much more popular than anticipated, and this painting was one of its stars. Holbein, originally active as a painter in Basel, settled in England, where he specialised in portraits of courtiers and prominent citizens. A document dated 1536 reveals that he was working as court painter to Henry VIII at the time he executed this work.

An inscription in the striking blue background of this portrait identifies the sitter: Robert Cheseman, an English nobleman who held the position of king's falconer. Cheseman holds a hunting falcon that is so beautifully rendered that it almost upstages the man himself. Holbein captured both the fierceness of the hawk – the largest hunting falcon, known as a gyrofalcon – with its gripping claws and hunting gear, but also the softness of the downy white breast feathers that Cheseman is stroking. The sitter is also a powerful presence, with his strong features, rich clothes and dignified, somewhat dreamy expression.

How did such a quintessentially English painting end up in The Hague? Since childhood, the Dutch Stadholder and English King William III loved falconry. In about 1700 he transferred this painting, along with another portrait by Holbein of an English nobleman with a hawk, to his hunting lodge, Het Loo Palace in Apeldoorn. After the death of William III, Queen Anne of England tried in vain to reclaim Holbein's paintings. They were eventually transferred to the Mauritshuis in 1822 as part of the stadholders' art collection.

ESEMAN . . ETATIS . SVÆ . XLVIII
DM · M . D . XXXIII ·

Jan Brueghel the Elder and Peter Paul Rubens
Brussels 1568–1625 Antwerp; Siegen 1577–1640 Antwerp

The Garden of Eden with the Fall of Man, *c.*1617
Oil on panel, 74 × 114 cm
Acquired by Prince William V, 1766
MH 253

Much as video-artists or film-makers today work in a team, this picture was the result of a collaboration between two painters: Peter Paul Rubens and his colleague Jan Brueghel the Elder. In the seventeenth century it was not unusual for artists to work together, and this panel is an outstanding example of such work. It represents the Garden of Eden at the moment that Eve, having accepted the forbidden fruit from the serpent, gives it to Adam.

Brueghel, a specialist in highly detailed landscapes populated with people and animals, painted the background first, leaving an area at the left empty so that Rubens could add the figures of Adam and Eve, the serpent, the horse and part of the tree. It is likely that the panel was then brought to Rubens' studio, where he inserted his part, then returned to Brueghel, who filled in gaps around the figures and added finishing touches. The resulting painting was a 'spectacle piece', intended to show off the artists' outstanding painting techniques.

The panel is in exceptionally good condition, so every detail is still visible. Brueghel filled the entire garden with plants, animals and insects. He had been able to observe some of the exotic animals at first hand in the menagerie of the Habsburg Archdukes Albert and Isabella. He rendered them with such life that the painting still delights the many schoolchildren who visit the Mauritshuis.

Peter Paul Rubens
Siegen 1577–1640 Antwerp

Old Woman and a Boy with Candles, *c.*1616–17

Oil on panel, 79 × 61 cm
Acquired with the support of the BankGiro Lottery, the Friends of the Mauritshuis Foundation, the Mondriaan Foundation, the Rembrandt Association (with the assistance of the Prince Bernhard Culture Fund) and a bequest from Ms A.A.W. Schröder, 2005.
MH 1150

This painting must have been very special to Rubens. An inventory of his art collection that was drawn up at his death on 30 May 1640 included this work, which tells us that Rubens kept it in his studio from the time it was made. It was painted on a panel that looks like a patchwork of planks – three vertical, one horizontal and four narrow strips along the sides – probably composed of inexpensive, remnant pieces of timber. There was evidently no need to lavish money on a painting that was to remain in the workshop anyway.

While Rubens was in Italy (from 1600 to 1608) he encountered the work of Caravaggio, characterised by a strong *chiaroscuro* (light and dark contrasts) and humble figures set close to the picture frame against a simple background. This painting, executed shortly after Rubens' return to Antwerp, is one of the earliest works produced in Caravaggio's style in the Netherlands.

Its subject matter is something of a mystery. A print made after the work appeared shortly after 1617, furnished by Rubens with a quotation from the Roman poet Ovid's *Ars Amatoria* ('Art of Love'). In it, Ovid describes an old woman who remembers her lost opportunities for love at night time. Here Rubens uses the candlelight to bring out the craggy skin and stooped pose of the old woman. A young boy, who seems to glow with youth and good health, lights his candle by hers – could she be passing along the wisdom gained with age to enjoy life and love while he still has his youth?

Anthony van Dyck
Antwerp 1599–1641 London

***Portrait of Anna Wake*, 1628; *Portrait of Peeter Stevens*, 1627**

Oil on canvas, 112.5 × 99.3 cm; oil on canvas, 112.5 × 99.4 cm

Acquired by Prince William V, 1768

MH 240; MH 239

There is something very unusual about this pair of portraits: namely their placement. Convention for pendant portraits dictated that the man should be on the left and his wife on the right. The usual order was reversed in this case, because the prosperous Antwerp cloth merchant and important collector Peeter Stevens had commissioned Anthony van Dyck to paint him in 1627. The pendant of his wife was an afterthought, added after his marriage to Anna Wake, the daughter of a fabulously wealthy merchant.

Van Dyck is an artist dear to my heart, particularly for the way that he represented dress. The son of a haberdasher and a mother who made complex embroidery, Van Dyck was well aware of the power of clothing to say something about his sitters, and contemporary remarks indicate that he dressed beautifully himself. In these portraits, Anna Wake and Peeter Stevens appear in black, but their attire is not at all sober. The gleaming silks, expensive lace, intricate embroidery and her ropes of pearls were all in the latest fashion and suitable dress for this 'power couple'. The way in which the figures are painted also marks them as a wealthy couple. They have the ease and self-assurance that accompanies those who have been well born. Van Dyck achieved this by giving them fluid, languid gestures and by taking a low perspective. We look up at them, as others in Antwerp would have done at the time.

Willem van Haecht
Antwerp 1593–1637 Antwerp

Apelles Painting Campaspe, *c.*1630
Oil on panel, 105 × 149.5 cm
Acquired by Prince William V, 1765
MH 266

The Mauritshuis is lucky to have a whole art gallery within this picture, a so-called *Kunstkamer* (cabinet picture) by the Flemish artist and curator Willem van Haecht. This is only one of three paintings by his hand, and shows his skill as a painter and connoisseur. He was registered in the Antwerp painters guild as a painter, but was also curator to Cornelis van de Geest, a prominent collector and one of Rubens' most important patrons.

This fictional art gallery forms a background for the story of Apelles and Campaspe, originally related by Pliny the Elder. Apelles, court painter to Alexander the Great, falls hopelessly in love when he has to paint a portrait of Campaspe, the king's most beautiful concubine. Alexander takes pity on the painter and rewards him for his excellent work by giving him Campaspe as his wife when the portrait is finished. The story was always a popular subject for artists, for whom Apelles personified the art of painting.

We can still identify many of the paintings that crowd this fictional art gallery, many of which now grace the walls of some of the most important museums in Europe. The large picture on the lower tier of the wall behind the figures, for example, is *Battle of the Amazons*, which Rubens painted for Cornelis van der Geest around 1615 and which now hangs in the Alte Pinakothek, Munich. The sculpture gallery is based on that in Rubens' own house in Antwerp. Indeed, the entire picture is an ode to the success of the art and artists of Antwerp.

CLARA · PEETERS

Clara Peeters
Antwerp active 1607/8–c.1621

Still Life with Cheese, Almonds and Pretzels, c.1615

Oil on panel, 34.5 × 49.5 cm

Acquired with the support of the Friends of the Mauritshuis Foundation, the BankGiro Lottery, the Rembrandt Association (with the assistance of its A.M. Roeters van Lennep Fund, Utrecht Rembrandt Circle and the Caius Circle) and a private donor, 2012

MH 1203

Ironically, for a painting of inanimate objects, this still life seems to sparkle with life. Surfaces are carefully rendered to show their variety of textures and the reflection of light. On the left are a pile of three different cheeses topped by a dish of butter shavings. Next to these are an earthenware jug with a pewter top and a covered Venetian wine glass in front of a bread roll. In the foreground on the well-worn table are two pretzels, a silver knife and a delicate Chinese porcelain dish holding almonds, raisins and figs.

We know little about Clara Peeters, a female artist active in Antwerp in the seventeenth century, but she gives us some hints through the objects in this painting. A tiny reflection in the lid of the earthenware jug is, in fact, a self-portrait. Peeters also inscribed her own name on the edge of the silver knife, which also bears the Antwerp silversmiths' mark, and was probably a wedding gift.

This painting more than meets the Mauritshuis' strict criteria for acquisitions, and we were delighted to buy it from an American private collection in 2012. Soon after its acquisition, the staff of the Mauritshuis began to call this work 'Clara' and referred to it affectionately as 'she'. Only one other painting in the collection has a similar honour, and that is Vermeer's *Girl with a Pearl Earring* (see pp.76–7)

Pieter van Anraadt
Utrecht *c.*1635–1678 Deventer

Still Life with Earthenware Jug and Pipes, 1658

Oil on canvas, 67 × 58.8 cm

Acquired with the support of the Friends of the Mauritshuis Foundation, the Prince Bernhard Cultural Foundation and the Rembrandt Association, 1972

MH 1045

The Mauritshuis not only collects works by famous names but also outstanding works by more obscure artists. This painting of astonishing quality is by an artist who has been largely forgotten outside specialist circles. Van Anraadt trained in Utrecht and had modest success in Amsterdam early in his career. He spent most of his career in Deventer, however, where he produced ordinary portraits of local dignitaries – nothing nearly as subtle as this still life.

This type of still life would have been known as a 'beer and tobacco piece' in the seventeenth century. It depicts a Westerwald stoneware jug, a glass of beer, an earthenware vessel full of hot coals and a pewter plate with pipes and tobacco wrapped in an old piece of paper, all displayed on a wooden table partly covered with a green cloth. There is no clear underlying meaning in this work. Although attitudes toward smoking in seventeenth-century Holland varied – some praised it for its supposed medicinal value, while others thought it a dissolute and addictive habit – everyone was familiar with the paraphernalia. People commonly drank beer at all mealtimes, including breakfast, because it was cleaner and safer than ordinary water. All in all, there is nothing remarkable about the objects on display. What is unusual is Van Anraadt's ability to capture the play of light on these humble objects, making them seem as tactile and real as if they had just been placed before us.

Adriaen Coorte
Middelburg (?) active *c.*1683–1707

Still Life with Strawberries, 1705
Oil on paper over panel, 16.5 × 14 cm
Gift of Mrs Edward Speelman in memory of Mr Edward Speelman
MH 1106

Until several decades ago the name Adriaen Coorte was virtually unknown, but his star has risen. Coorte is now one of the artists most sought-after by collectors, and his work commands high prices on the art market. We know little about him except that he worked as a painter from 1683 until 1707, probably in Middelburg in the province of Zeeland. He may well have been self-taught, as he never entered the guild. Coorte specialised in still lifes like this one, mostly small in format and showing fruits or vegetables laid out on the edge of a table against a plain, dark background.

This tiny postcard-sized work was painted on paper and subsequently pasted down on panel, as were many of Coorte's still lifes. The artist signed and dated the work 1705 on the edge of the table. The composition is simple, but it is carefully composed to create an uncanny balance. To us the strawberries look like wild ones, but they were actually the only kind on offer in the Netherlands at the time. The white flower rises above the pile of strawberries, contrasting with the horizontal line of the table and the low pile of fruit. Coorte often illuminated surfaces slightly to one side, so that the edges of the leaves and stems stand out starkly against the plain background, almost as if backlit. That same light strikes the bumps and seeds of the strawberries in such a way as to bring out their roundness and texture. These strawberries, so different from the large ones we usually eat today, seem full of flavour and very, very tempting.

Ambrosius Bosschaert the Elder
Antwerp 1573–1621 The Hague

Vase with Flowers in a Window, *c.*1618

Oil on panel, 64 × 46 cm

Bequest of Arnoldus des Tombe, 1903

MH 679

How deceptive Dutch still lifes can be. This glorious bouquet, made up in a handsome glass vase, is placed on a window ledge before a deep, imaginary landscape. We can identify each of the thirty different types of flower included, from the variegated iris at the top of the bouquet to the carnation on the ledge. This could never have existed, however, because the flowers do not come out at the same time of year. Bosschaert carefully constructed a very symmetrical arrangement of colourful flowers based on his own botanical studies. Indeed, the same plants appear in some of his other works, and he seems to have drawn on paintings by other artists as well. He rendered the flowers, shells and insects in tiny brushstrokes, so smooth that this oil painting looks like a miniature on vellum.

Spurred on by the growing interest in botany, flower pieces were immensely popular in the seventeenth century, and Bosschaert's paintings fetched very high prices. The artist spent most of his career in Middelburg – the same town where Coorte was to make his strawberries at a later date – with an enthusiastic following of amateur botanists who were happy to pay handsome prices for his work; he also sold paintings to courtiers in The Hague. Buying a painting such as this is out of the question today, but many of our visitors take home a reproduction of the glass vase in this work, which we call the 'Bosschaert vase', from our museum shop.

Dirck de Bray
Haarlem *c.*1635–1694 Goch

***Still Life with a Bouquet in the Making*, 1674**

Oil on panel, 40.5 cm × 35.7 cm
Acquired with the support of the BankGiro Lottery, the Rembrandt Association and a private benefactor, 2011
MH 1166

This is the kind of painting that suits the Mauritshuis perfectly: an outstanding work by a lesser-known Dutch artist, which is in excellent condition, small in scale, rich in detail and a real addition to the collection. The acquisition of this sublime flower painting was a great coup. It had been on the museum's wish-list for many years, but its owner loved it deeply and did not want to part with it. Circumstances changed, and we were able to buy it for the collection in 2011.

This is a highly unusual flower painting for the period. Works by Dirck de Bray, the maker of only seven extant flower still lifes, are very rare. The composition is also very unusual, as the bouquet is not yet finished – roughly half of the flowers are still laid out on the stone table. Unlike the flowers in Bosschaert's painting, these all bloom at the same time in the spring. The charming arrangement has a casual quality and a freshness that seems ahead of its time and anticipates the eighteenth century.

This painting, like most of those in the Mauritshuis, is in outstanding condition. Before acquiring it, we examined the picture out of its frame under good light. Our Head of Conservation noticed a slight ding in the panel, about one-third of the way down in the right-hand background. The artist must have seen that too, as he took advantage of the imperfection to transform it into a tiny spider, lowering itself on a silken thread.

Thomas de Keyser
Amsterdam 1596/7–1667 Amsterdam

Portrait of Loef Vredericx as an Ensign, 1626

Oil on panel, 92.5 × 69 cm

Acquired with the support of the Rembrandt Association and private benefactors, 1931

MH 806

I can think of no better expression of pride than this portrait. The sitter, Loef Vredericx, who can be identified by an inscription on the back of the panel, was a prominent silversmith in Amsterdam. He was appointed to the position of ensign in Amsterdam's civic guard in 1626. Membership of this volunteer militia was reserved for residents of good standing, and the ensign had to fulfil particular requirements: to be unmarried, young and strong enough to carry the heavy standard and to come from a good family. Loef Vredericx celebrated his prestigious appointment by commissioning the most prominent Amsterdam portraitist of his day to paint him dressed in his finery. Ensigns were always the most richly and colourfully dressed members of a civic guard. This full-length portrait, unusual in Holland, also expresses Loef Vredericx's pride in his country and city. The Amsterdam coat-of-arms is just visible over the doorway, and the Dutch lion and the text *pro patria* ('for the fatherland') decorate the standard. More telling than any of these accessories, however, is the proud bearing and expression of the man himself.

The painting entered the collection of the Mauritshuis in a very unusual way. Wilhelm Martin, a former director of the Mauritshuis, travelled to Russia in 1924. He encountered this portrait on the estate of Gatchina near St Petersburg and was able to attribute it to De Keyser on the basis of a monogram above the door. When the Bolsheviks sold off large numbers of paintings from the national collections around 1930, Martin snapped this up for the museum.

Frans Hals
Antwerp 1582/3–1666 Haarlem

Laughing Boy, *c.*1625
Oil on panel, diameter 30.4 cm
Acquired with the support of the Rembrandt Association, the Prince Bernhard Culture Fund and the Friends of the Mauritshuis Foundation, 1968
MH 1032

Frans Hals is best known as a portrait painter, famous for the rough and free brushwork displayed so well here. This small circular panel was not intended to show a particular person. Instead, it is the study of a facial expression: pure joy. The young boy smiles radiantly, and his entire being seems to shine and bounce with pleasure. Highly unusually for a Dutch painting, the boy's expression reveals his teeth. These might be a bit brown by today's standards, but nothing could dampen his happiness.

Marie-Anne Friedländer-Fuld, Baroness de Goldschmidt-Rothschild sold this painting to the Mauritshuis in 1968 with a condition attached. She had bought the painting in 1918 as a young woman and had become very attached to it. She insisted, therefore, on keeping it for nine months a year until her death, so it could only be put on display in the museum for the remaining three months. Between 1968 and 1973, the director of the Mauritshuis travelled to Paris twice a year to fetch the painting and return it. I would have been happy to do so if I had been in his place, because the work has become one of the icons of the collection, a firm favourite of staff and visitors alike.

Jacob van Campen
Haarlem 1596–1657 Amersfoort

***Double Portrait of Constantijn Huygens and Suzanna van Baerle**, c.1635*

Oil on canvas, 95 × 78.5 cm

Acquired by the Friends of the Mauritshuis Foundation with the support of private benefactors, 1992

MH 1089

This portrait's subjects and painter are closely linked to the Mauritshuis. Because of this, it was the subject of a public campaign to help the museum acquire it shortly after its rediscovery. My predecessor, Frits Duparc, was able to add this important painting to the collection of the Mauritshuis in 1992 with the support of the museum's friends and many private donors.

The sitters are Constantijn Huygens and his wife Suzanna van Baerle. Huygens was secretary to three successive stadholders – Frederik Hendrik, Willem II and Willem III – and played a key role in the political and cultural life of The Hague for much of the seventeenth century. Well known as a musician and poet, he was also a connoisseur of painting and architecture. The artist is Jacob van Campen, a man of many talents, known mainly as an architect who also designed the Mauritshuis, the construction of which Huygens oversaw while Johan Maurits was in Brazil. Indeed, Huygens' own house was also designed by Van Campen and was located across the street from the Mauritshuis; unfortunately, it was demolished in the nineteenth century.

Many images of Huygens survive, but this is the only double portrait with his beloved wife. It is highly unusual that one of the sitters is shown in profile and the other looks directly at the viewer. Huygens expressed his love for Suzanna in many of his poems and nicknamed her 'Sterre' (Star). In this portrait, the couple hold a musical score that illustrates the harmony of their marriage. Sadly, this happy union ended with her untimely death in 1637.

Caesar van Everdingen
Alkmaar 1617/18–1678 Alkmaar

Diogenes Looking for an Honest Man
(or ***Portait historié of the Steyn Family***), 1652

Oil on canvas, 75.9 × 103.6 cm

Bequest of Cornelia Steyn-Schellinger to Prince William V, 1783

MH 39

There are no two ways about it: this is a very odd picture. A family portrait, a history painting and the *dernier cri* of Dutch Classicism, all rolled into one. This is a so-called *portrait historié*, in other words a portrait showing actual people playing the role of historical figures. The story is that of the Greek philosopher Diogenes, who strolled through the Athens market in broad daylight with a lit lamp. When asked why, he replied that he was searching for an honest man. Diogenes propagated a simple way of life, alluded to here by his modest dress and the turnips in the wheelbarrow to the left. Diogenes reappears in the background to the left, seated in the barrel that he made his home. The man in the turban leaning over him is Alexander the Great, who promises to give him anything he wants, but Diogenes only wants him to stop blocking his sunlight. The two dogs in the foreground refer to Diogenes' sect the Cynics, which literally means 'canines'.

The men, women and children in the foreground have been identified as members of the prominent and wealthy Steyn family from Haarlem. The couple wearing black sixteenth-century costumes at the right are posthumous portraits of the family's forebears, somewhat eerily included with their descendants in the scene. The story is set in a very Dutch marketplace that looks like the Grote Markt in Haarlem, but this has been altered with classicising embellishments and fictitious details. The composition, with its frieze of figures in the foreground, is also typical of Dutch Classicist painting.

Adriaen Hanneman
The Hague *c.*1604–1671 The Hague

Posthumous Portrait of Mary Stuart (1631–1660) with a Servant, *c.*1664
Oil on canvas, 129.5 × 119.3 cm
Acquired in or before 1875
MH 429

Portraits make up about half of the Mauritshuis' collection, but this one stands out for its exoticism. The subject is Mary Stuart, daughter of Charles I of England and wife of Stadholder William II. She was not the only Englishwoman to settle in The Hague. Elizabeth Stuart, Charles I's sister and the wife of the so-called 'Winter King', Elector Frederik V, also lived there, and many other English expatriates joined them during the Civil War (1642–51). Adriaen Hanneman spent time working in London, where he was strongly influenced by Anthony van Dyck and may even have worked in his studio. Hanneman became a favourite of the English community in The Hague for his sophisticated compositions, which had a flavour of the English court.

This painting was executed some years after Mary Stuart's death, probably in around 1664. She appears in an unusual costume, one that would have been worn at a court pageant known as a masque. The colourful mantle, held into place at her shoulder by a large jewelled clasp, is made of South American feathers. On her head she wears a large turban hung with a strand of large pearls and topped with more red feathers. These items were probably made in Europe with feathers brought from Brazil by Johan Maurits. As well as bags of feathers, he brought home similar mantles that had been made in Brazil, five of which are still kept in the National Museum of Denmark. The black page at Mary Stuart's side, a trope derived from Van Dyck, further strengthens the exoticism of the image.

Johannes Thopas
Arnhem *c.*1625–*c.*1690–5 Assendelft

Portrait of a Deceased Girl, Probably Catharina Margaretha van Valkenburg, *c.*1682
Oil on panel, 59 × 71 cm
Acquired by the Friends of the Mauritshuis Foundation, 2008
MH 1159

As the first female director of the Mauritshuis, my first acquisition was of this painting. It seems horribly inappropriate, but this picture was acquired on its own merit and in spite of the gruesome subject. It had remained among the possessions of the Van Valkenburg family for more than three centuries and was largely unknown until it appeared in an exhibition in 1998. In fact, it is the only extant painting by the artist Johannes Thopas, who is otherwise known for his detailed portrait drawings. This is surprising, since he must have made more paintings to achieve the high level of skill shown here. The portrait is undoubtedly the best-preserved example of a deathbed portrait extant today, and its plush red velvet curtains and shiny satin coverlet make it the most colourful.

Portraits of children who had slipped away were not at all rare in an age of high infant mortality rates. That did not make the loss any more bearable for the parents, and so portraits such as this were commissioned in order to keep the memory of the child alive. X-rays reveal that Thopas had originally painted the little girl with clasped hands, as was more conventional for such a portrait, but he altered this to give her a more natural pose. She has rosy cheeks and freshly plumped up pillows, more like a girl asleep than a corpse on her deathbed. At least, that is what I like to think.

Joachim Wtewael
Utrecht 1566–1638 Utrecht

Mars and Venus Surprised by Vulcan, 1601

Oil on copper, 20.8 × 15.7 cm

Acquired for the Stadholder's collection, before 1757

MH 223

Seventeenth-century painters aspired to work on histories – stories from mythology or the Bible – which were considered the most prestigious specialty. Wtewael was a successful history painter, and this work is a particularly exciting example. It relates the story of Mars and Venus, as told by Homer and Ovid. Venus is married to Vulcan, but she has an affair with Mars. When Vulcan discovers this, he forges a net of very fine bronze, which he spreads over Venus' bed, and literally catches Mars and Venus in the act. Vulcan gathers them up and shows them to the assembled gods, who are amused by the episode. Mercury even admits he would willingly take the place of Mars with Venus in bed.

Wtewael's muscled and twisted figures are typical of a style called Mannerism. He painted this work, which is still in outstanding condition, on a tiny copper plate. This hard and durable surface is perfect for painting in great detail with a fine technique. The small size of this work had another advantage. Its eroticism is so frank that the painting was frequently hidden away. The 1757 inventory of Het Loo Palace, where the painting was kept at the time, states that it was stored in a small cupboard. Shorty before 1900, the director of the Mauritshuis also decided it was too racy to put on display and put it in store. In 1929 it was still not on view because 'an immature public needed to be protected from itself'. How times have changed.

Rembrandt van Rijn
Leiden 1606–1669 Amsterdam

Simeon's Song of Praise, 1631

Oil on panel, 60.9 × 47.9 cm

Acquired by Prince William IV, 1733

MH 145

Rembrandt is justly famous for so many aspects of his work, but this painting demonstrates his uncanny ability as a narrative painter especially well. Rembrandt infallibly chose the most telling moment in a story and always managed to capture its most emotional, human element. Rembrandt painted this Biblical work when he was still a young artist, before achieving great success in Amsterdam. It tells the story of Simeon as related in the Gospel of St Luke. After their child's circumcision, Mary and Joseph went to the temple in Jerusalem to dedicate their firstborn to the Lord and to make the obligatory sacrifice of two young turtle doves. Simeon, a just and devout man, had been informed that he should not die before he had seen Christ. When Mary and Joseph came to the temple, Simeon took the child in his arms, blessed God and said, 'Lord now lettest thou thy servant depart in peace, according to thy word: For mine eyes have seen thy salvation'(Luke 2:25).

Although the panel is small, Rembrandt cleverly used light and dark to create a monumental space. He chose the most tender moment of the episode – when Simeon looks up to praise the Lord. Simeon kneels in a pool of light that refers directly to the text and evokes divine revelation. Mary and Joseph, holding two doves, kneel beside him looking on in astonishment. The oversized figure standing with arms raised is probably the Prophetess Anna, who looms over the other figures, making them seem even more vulnerable and human. Figures from all walks of life are arranged in tiers throughout the temple. Everyone seems to be watching closely and participating, and so do we as viewers.

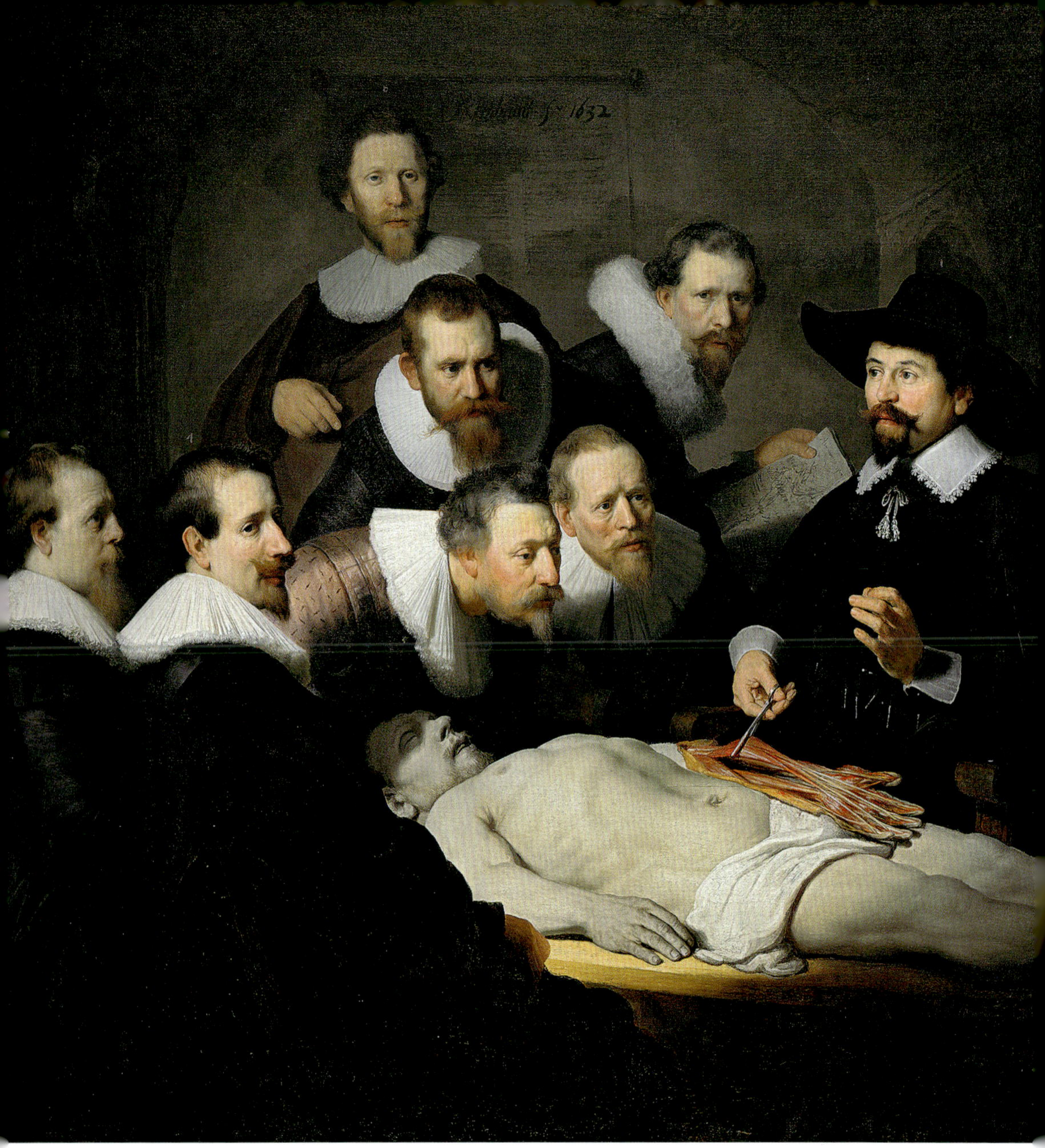

Rembrandt van Rijn
Leiden 1606–1669 Amsterdam

The Anatomy Lesson of Dr Nicolaes Tulp, 1632

Oil on canvas, 169 × 216.5 cm

Acquired in 1828

MH 146

Rembrandt made his breakthrough in Amsterdam with this painting, and it has been one of his most renowned works ever since. It is a group portrait of the Amsterdam surgeons' guild. Rembrandt created a thrilling presentation by means of strong light and dark contrasts and a clever composition, with the corpse displayed at an angle. The head of the guild (*Praelector*) is Dr Nicolaes Tulp, shown here giving the demonstration. All of the other members, who can still be identified on the basis of documents, are actively engaged, and some even lean in to get a closer look. The effect is one of such immediacy that you feel as if you are standing in the theatre as another member of the group.

Rembrandt veered substantially from the truth in order to achieve such a dramatic portrait. Anatomy lessons would have been held for a very large audience, not such a small group. The demonstration would have started with the bowels, to minimise the smell. Tulp's pose and the deconstructed forearm are not drawn from life, but from a portrait of the Flemish anatomist Andreas Vesalius from his important book on anatomy. The body made available for this demonstration was that of a criminal known as Aris Kindt, who had been sentenced to death for robbery and hanged. Kindt, who was an inveterate thief, had lost his right hand as a result of a previous conviction. X-rays show that Rembrandt originally painted a stump, but later decided to paint a hand over it, which has discoloured slightly with age.

REMBRANDT VAN RIJN
Leiden 1606–1669 Amsterdam

Self-portrait, 1669

Oil on canvas, 63.5 × 57.8 cm
Acquired with the support of the Rembrandt Association and private benefactors, 1947
MH 840

REMBRANDT PRODUCED SO MANY self-portraits during his career that his face has become almost as familiar as that of a family member. This painting shows Rembrandt at the end of his life, his skin sagging, pouches under his eyes, but as alert as ever. The virtuoso handling of this painting is completely unlike Rembrandt's earlier *Simeon* and *The Anatomy Lesson* (see pp.44–5 and 46–7) and typical of his late style. The complex build-up of many layers makes it a truly three-dimensional object, which manages to be strikingly alive. An X-ray has shown that Rembrandt first painted himself wearing a white cap of a type commonly worn by painters for studio use. At a later stage, he transformed this into a rich turban with just a few fluid strokes of his brush.

This self-portrait was long believed to be the only one Rembrandt made in 1669, the last year of his life. Many thought they could read in it an expression of melancholy and exhaustion. Then the same date was discovered on another self-portrait in the National Gallery in London, one in which no one had ever seen signs of Rembrandt's imminent death. Since then a third self-portrait dated 1669 has been discovered in the Galleria degli Uffizi, Florence. This is a cautionary tale of how easy it is for art historians to project onto an image ideas that may in fact have little to do with the truth.

Carel Fabritius
Midden-Beemster 1622–1654 Delft

The Goldfinch, 1654

Oil on panel, 33.5 × 22.8

Acquired in 1896

MH 605

Fabritius used broad and free brushstrokes, sometimes thickly layered, to create an extraordinary illusion of a real bird. The artist included enough detail to allow us to recognise the bird, which is chained to its feeding box, as a European goldfinch (*Carduelis carduelis*). Known fondly in Dutch as a *puttertje* ('water-drawer') for its ability to draw water from a bowl or glass using a tiny bucket on a chain, this bird was a popular pet. Why and for whom Fabritius painted this little work remains a puzzle. Its support is a fairly thick panel, sawn from a larger one. Scholars have speculated that it may have been made to form part of a cage or piece of furniture. We cannot be sure how it was meant to be used, but it was certainly intended as a *trompe l'oeuil* painting, one intended to fool the eye, and as such it is certainly successful. The perspective of the box, the shadow cast on the rough, plaster wall and the bird's pert expression all contribute to the extraordinary illusion that the bird is alive and singing its heart out.

Fabritius, who signed and dated this small panel in the year of his death, had worked in Rembrandt's studio in Amsterdam and later settled in Delft. He died tragically when a gunpowder magazine exploded in the city, setting off an enormous fire. Most of Fabritius' paintings also perished in that blaze, so this is not only a much-loved and charming work but also a very rare one.

Gerrit Dou
Leiden 1613–1675 Leiden

The Young Mother, 1658

Oil on panel (rounded at top), 73.5 × 55.5 cm
Acquired by the Stadholder-King William III, after 1688
MH 32

Dou was, like Fabritius, closely associated with Rembrandt, but at an earlier stage in Rembrandt's career when he was still living and working in Leiden. Dou stayed in Leiden and developed into what we now call a fine-painter (*fijnschilder*), a specialist in pictures that had a mirror-smooth surface full of detail. Here a young woman sits next to an open window in a spacious room with high ceilings. She looks up from her needlework, while a young girl kneels beside a wicker cradle with a sleeping baby. The figures and some of the objects in the foreground are bathed in sunlight. The background is gloomy, but we can just make out a kitchen with a few figures. All sorts of household objects are scattered throughout the space, each painted in painstaking detail. We call a scene such as this, which seems to be a snapshot of everyday life, a genre painting. This is not an exact representation of an actual scene, but it looks as if it might have been.

The Young Mother once hung next to Rembrandt's *Simeon* (see pp.44–5) in Het Loo Palace. It is probable that the English King Charles II knew Dou's painting from his time in exile in The Hague. When he returned to England as king in 1660 the states of Holland and West Friesland decided to honour him with a diplomatic gift. They sent a formidable group of paintings, including this one. It was one of the stars of the Royal Collection in England until Stadholder William III, who had become King of England in 1689, brought it back to the Netherlands.

Nicolaes Maes
Dordrecht 1634–1693 Amsterdam

The Old Lacemaker, *c.*1655

Oil on panel, 37.5 × 35 cm
Acquired with the support of the Friends of the Mauritshuis Foundation, the VSB Fund for The Hague and Environs and the Rembrandt Association, 1994
MH 1101

Like the painting by Gerrit Dou, this is also a genre painting by a Rembrandt pupil, but this has an entirely different character and atmosphere. Rembrandt must have been a talented teacher, since his pupils developed in such a great variety of directions. Nicolaes Maes began as history painter, then returned to his birthplace, Dordrecht, where he generally painted genre scenes such as this, and eventually ended up painting slick small-scale society portraits in Amsterdam. We now love him best for his genre paintings, which show women and girls engaged in domestic activities. Rembrandt's influence is still visible in the strong contrasts of light and dark as well as the sympathetic depiction of the people in these scenes.

The space in this painting is divided neatly into two halves. To the left is a wonderful still life of gleaming earthenware pots and other utensils. To the right sits an old woman making bobbin lace, absorbed in her task. Diligence and concentration, which are necessary for complex work such as hers, were seen as virtues in the seventeenth century. Maes signed his name prominently on the woman's foot warmer, but he need not have done so. The tints of warm, orangey red and brown are so characteristic of this artist that the painting could not be by anyone else.

Gerard ter Borch
Zwolle 1617–1681 Deventer

***Woman Writing a Letter*, c.1655**

Oil on panel, 39 × 29.5 cm
Gift of Sir Henri Deterding, 1928
MH 797

Like the painting by Maes, this is a domestic interior showing a woman on her own, which is also dominated by a subtle play of reds, but that is where the similarity ends. This is not a simple kitchen but an elegant interior, which is furnished with a canopy bed and a table partially covered with a valuable Oriental carpet. The young woman sits at the table writing a letter, using the pewter ink set next to her. She wears a satin bodice decorated with gold brocade, a fashionable hairstyle and a large pearl earring with a blue ribbon. Everything in this scene – from the activity of writing to the costly clothing and furniture – mark this as a domain of the well off. This type of elegant interior showing a woman quietly engaged in an activity inspired other artists, among them Johannes Vermeer and Frans van Mieris the Elder, to produce similar works.

Letter writing was very popular in Ter Borch's time, and the Dutch female population had one of the highest literacy rates in Western Europe. Here the writing paper has been folded in two and is already covered with writing, so presumably the woman is going over what she has already set down. As much as we would like to believe she is writing a love letter, we cannot be sure. In any event, it is hard to believe that her prose is not as elegant as her appearance.

Jan Steen
Leiden 1626–1679 Leiden

'As the Old Sing, so Pipe the Young', *c.*1665
Oil on canvas, 134 × 163 cm
Acquired with the support of the Rembrandt Association, 1913
MH 742

The best known of the Dutch genre painters is undoubtedly the humorous Jan Steen, and he is most famous for this type of unruly household scene. In fact, the Dutch phrase 'a Jan Steen household' aptly describes a particularly messy and chaotic family life. This entire scene revolves around the grandmother seated at the table in the centre, who is singing from a song-sheet. Its title is clearly legible and is in translation: 'As the old sing, so pipe the young'. This painting offers the moralising lesson that, for better or for worse, the young learn from the example set by adults – in this case a very bad example. The man in the hat just to the right of centre is Jan Steen himself, whom we know from the many self-portraits he produced. He is teaching the young boy to smoke a pipe. As if to underscore the expression '…so pipe the young', a boy behind them plays the bagpipes. The parrot in the background to the left also alludes to the theme of learning and imitation. The mother, who is seated in the foreground and has clearly had a glass too many, accepts more wine. Behind her sits the grandfather, wearing a hat that would have been worn at the baptism of a child; Steen is possibly calling into question the paternity of the child. As always, Steen does not lay the moralising on with a trowel but gives his scene humour and fun.

Jan Steen
Leiden 1626–1679 Leiden

Girl Offering Oysters (or ***Oyster Eater***), *c.*1658–60

Oil on panel, 20.5 × 145.5 cm

Gift of Sir Henri Deterding, 1936

MH 818

The Mauritshuis has a very large painting by Jan Steen (see pp.58–9) and also his smallest. This tiny work looks like a miniature and is painted as if it were the work of a fine-painter. A young woman, who is richly clad in a fur-trimmed velvet jacket, has sat down to a meal of oysters. Steen created a marvellous little still life on the table before her, complete with a jug and glass of wine as well as a silver tray with salt, a cone of pepper and a half-eaten loaf of bread. Oysters are spread across the table cloth, and a couple of servants in the kitchen behind her open more.

The young woman sprinkles a little bit of salt on the oyster in her hand and looks out directly from the picture with a saucy expression. No wonder, since oysters were considered aphrodisiacs in the seventeenth century, as they sometimes still are today. There is no man with whom she can share her exciting meal, so she looks straight out, appealing to us. Steen hit the message home by placing a canopy bed behind her. As my professor in graduate school once said, 'She's just like a pin-up girl'.

Hendrik Avercamp
Amsterdam 1585–1634 Kampen

On the Ice, *c.*1610
Oil on panel, 36 × 71 cm
On long-term loan from the Rijksmuseum, Amsterdam, since 1924
MH 785

From about 1550 to 1850 Holland experienced a period of very cold winters and relatively cool summers. During the winter waterways froze and roads were covered with snow, making usual routes impassable, and recreation moved onto the ice. No artist could depict these winters better than Avercamp, who became a specialist in drawing and painting typically Dutch scenes of people enjoying the cold outdoors.

Avercamp shows the vista across a frozen canal in a peasant village. We can see far into the frozen landscape, which has leaden skies and an indescribably cold, dark and damp atmosphere. Even so, the villagers have come out of their houses to amuse themselves. Avercamp filled every corner of this scene with meticulously rendered figures. The fashionable young man in a yellow-satin doublet, black-plumed hat, red sash and matching stockings skates expertly in the centre foreground. Around him are figures with long sticks playing *kolf* (an early game that combined elements of ice hockey and golf). In the middle ground is a group of young women, one of whom has tipped over and is exposing her bare behind. Some have fallen through the ice near the left bank and are about to be rescued. No matter how many times you see this painting, it keeps offering new and amusing details.

Paulus Potter
Enkhuizen 1625–1654 Amsterdam

The Bull, 1647

Oil on canvas, 235.5 × 339 cm

Acquired by Prince William IV, 1749

MH 136

In the nineteenth century it was this painting that made the Mauritshuis famous, much more so than the paintings by Vermeer and Rembrandt. It was held up as a paragon of Dutch painting for its striking naturalism and was admired for its large format (it is the biggest in the Mauritshuis collection).

To me, the painting always calls to mind an anecdote about a visitor to a ranch in Texas. As he sat down to dinner in the wood-panelled dining room, he noticed a series of oil paintings on the wall, all showing prize bulls. The host asked him if he was enjoying his steak, to which he politely replied that it was delicious. The host then pointed at one of the paintings with his knife: 'See that?' The guest nodded, and the host then pointed to the steaks on their plates and remarked with some pride, 'That's him!'

We might imagine that, like the Texas rancher, a proud farmer commissioned a life-sized portrait of his best bull from Potter, but nothing could be further from the truth. Various parts of the animal do not, in fact, fit together. The horns and the dewlap are characteristic of an animal around two years of age; the large, permanent teeth make the animal three or four; the forequarters are well developed, but the hindquarters are lean and smooth; and the perspective is not correct. We can conclude that this a very clever fabrication, one made in the artist's studio on the basis of various studies from life, and so it could not have been the portrait of a prize bull.

Jacob van Ruisdael
Haarlem 1628/9–1682 Amsterdam

View of Haarlem with Bleaching Fields, *c.*1670–5
Oil on canvas, 55.5 × 62 cm
Acquired in 1827
MH 155

Jacob van Ruisdael is undoubtedly the most important Dutch landscapist of his time, an artist who tirelessly explored ways of depicting the flat countryside, atmosphere and skies of his native land. This painting, which shows the landscape behind the dunes near Haarlem and Alkmaar, is of a type described as a *Haarlempje* ('little Haarlem') in seventeenth-century inventories. Ruisdael painted at least fifteen similar scenes, but this is one of the most evocative. He chose the viewpoint from the dunes, a high vantage point from which to show fields and the city of Haarlem on the horizon. Ruisdael devoted two-thirds of the composition to a characteristic Dutch sky, filled with cumulus clouds scudding rapidly overhead. The sun pours through gaps in these clouds, creating pools of light that pick out elements in the landscape.

In the foreground people are spreading out long strips of linen to bleach in the sunlight. Linen processing was, along with beer-making, one of Haarlem's most important industries. It was a time-consuming process that took two to three months and involved steeping the fabric in lye, rinsing it and spreading it onto fields where it was rinsed repeatedly with dune water. I once gave an eminent visitor from Ireland a tour of the collection, and her reaction to this painting surprised me. She cried out, 'Oh, I can still smell it!' Apparently, the bleaching industry was still very much alive when she was a small girl living outside Belfast, and she told me the smell was unbearable. For her, Ruisdael managed not only to evoke the appearance and atmosphere of the landscape around Haarlem, but also its smell.

Simon de Vlieger
Rotterdam (?) *c.*1601–1653 Weesp

Beach View, 1643
Oil on panel, 60.6 × 83.5 cm
Acquired in 1892
MH 558

The Netherlands is a coastal country where water is ever present – on inland waterways, at the sea or being held at bay to form polders, low lying areas of land that were reclaimed from the sea by means of dikes. In the seventeenth century the country was an international heavyweight in maritime trade. Not surprisingly, the sea and waterways figured prominently in landscape paintings, which often depicted the transitions between land and water. I have chosen this painting because it so beautifully captures the way the Dutch beach still looks today.

Simon de Vlieger, a specialist in marine paintings, usually used a broad range of colours. Here he uses a more limited palette with a subtle range of grey and brown hues to evoke the windswept beach and sea. Like Ruisdael, he devoted most of his painting to the sky, which is filled with threatening rain clouds. Only a few ships remain at sea; the rest seem to have come in close to the shore and moored on the beach. This beach is crowded with fishermen going about their daily tasks. A well-dressed couple with a dog and child stand on a dune in the foreground surveying the whole. You can almost feel the stiff breeze blowing across the scene.

Karel du Jardin
Amsterdam 1627–1678 Venice

Italian Landscape with a Young Shepherd Playing with his Dog, c.1660–5

Oil on panel, 31.2 × 37.6 cm
Gift of Jacques Goudstikker, 1919
MH 760

Artists such as Ruisdael and Potter concentrated on the beauty of the Dutch landscape and the people who lived there. Others looked to more exotic locations, in particular to Italy, for inspiration. Such a journey was far more common than we might think today and was considered *de rigueur* for any serious artist. In fact, the connoisseur Constantijn Huygens (see pp.34–5) criticised the young Rembrandt for ignoring advice to travel south. Most Dutch artists spent their time in Italy sketching the landscape and monuments. Almost all joined a society known as the *Bentvueghels*, which was the centre of what was, by all accounts, a raucous social life; they only began to paint seriously on returning home. One such painter was Karel du Jardin.

Du Jardin travelled to Italy more than once, but he made this lively painting in Amsterdam. The landscape could not be more different from Ruisdael's flat and watery depiction of Haarlem. There are no buildings or other signs of human life in this hilly countryside. It is awash with the golden light of Italy, which would have seemed exotic and warm to the Dutch. Above all, it is a joyous depiction of a young shepherd playing with his dog, his animals grazing peacefully alongside him in the late afternoon sunlight. It is not hard to imagine that this painting would have been particularly appealing to a collector during the dank and grey Dutch winter.

Frans Post
Haarlem *c.*1612–1680 Haarlem

View of the Island of Itamaracà, 1637
Oil on canvas, 63.5 × 88.5 cm
On long-term loan from the Rijksmuseum, Amsterdam, since 1953
MH 915

Like Du Jardin, Post painted a foreign landscape. This one, closely based on reality, was made in Brazil. Johan Maurits of Nassau-Siegen, the man who commissioned the building of the Mauritshuis, was appointed governor of the Dutch colony in Brazil by the Dutch West India Company, and today he is perhaps better known in Brazil than in the Netherlands. While he was governor, from 1636 to 1644, Johan Maurits put an end to Portuguese insurgencies and set about building a new capital, named Mauritsstad after its founder, and in so doing he created a climate in which trade could flourish. The success of trade, however, was due principally to the slave labour used on sugar plantations, whose crops were exported to the Dutch Republic. Johan Maurits was an enlightened governor who was interested in much more than economic and military success. He was genuinely curious about the local population and the indigenous plants and animals. He brought along scientists, who produced significant writings on Brazil, as well as the artists Frans Post and Albert Eckhout. Post painted true-to-life Brazilian landscapes with a naive charm. This painting, showing the island Itamaracà, is one of only seven surviving paintings that the artist made while he was in Brazil.

Johannes Vermeer
Delft 1632–1675 Delft

View of Delft, *c.*1660–1

Oil on canvas, 96.5 × 115.7 cm

Acquired in 1822

MH 92

The most important landscape in the collection is undoubtedly the *View of Delft* by Vermeer. To be more accurate, it is a cityscape, a view of the town in which Vermeer lived and worked. He chose a viewpoint from the southeast. We stand on the banks of the Schie Canal, looking towards a triangular harbour named the Kolk. The city itself is so accurately rendered that we can still identify all the buildings. In the background, just to the right of centre, stands the tower of the *Nieuwe Kerk* (New Church), spotlit by sunlight pouring through a break in the clouds. This would have been an incredibly busy waterway in Vermeer's day. Instead of painting the coming and going of boats and the movement of goods, Vermeer produced a scene that is utterly tranquil and harmonious. He altered the heights and relationships of buildings in order to achieve a perfectly balanced skyline. He made the figures in the foreground tiny, which gives the city an unexpected monumentality. The clouds and weather are dynamic – it seems as if a rain shower has just scrubbed the city – and yet all is still and quiet. Above all, it is the play of light on the different surfaces that makes this painting so special. I am often asked which painting from the collection of the Mauritshuis is my favourite. Although I love them all, when I am forced to choose, it is always this one.

JOHANNES VERMEER
Delft 1632–1675 Delft

Girl with a Pearl Earring, *c.*1665
Oil on canvas, 44.5 × 39 cm
Bequest of Arnoldus des Tombe, 1903
MH 670

IN THE PAST TWENTY YEARS or so, this painting has become the icon of the Mauritshuis. This is a recent development, resulting from the increased awareness and popularity of Vermeer, as well as the novel and the film based on this picture. Vermeer was a relatively unknown painter until his 'rediscovery' by French art critics in the nineteenth century. This painting came up for auction in The Hague in 1881, where it was recognised only by the influential art adviser Victor de Stuers and the collector Arnoldus des Tombe. They agreed not to bid against each other, and Des Tombe was able to buy it for the incredibly small amount of two guilders and thirty cents. Once it was cleaned, it became obvious that this was a great work by Vermeer, and the collector lent it to the Mauritshuis. Unknown to the Mauritshuis, Des Tombe left the painting to the museum in his will, and it has been part of the collection since 1903.

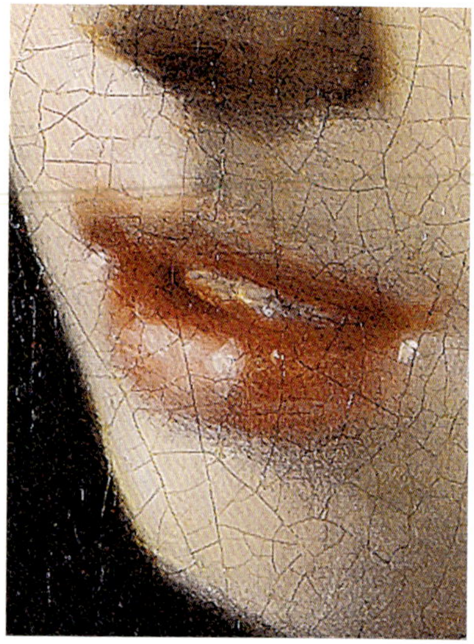

During the renovation and expansion of the Mauritshuis (2012–14), this painting travelled the world, visiting Tokyo, Kobe, San Francisco, Atlanta, New York and Bologna. Everywhere 'Girl' goes, she is a sensation. I am often at a loss to explain why this picture has such a universal appeal. The girl is obviously beautiful and sublimely painted in colours that are perfectly balanced. She is set against a dark background that seems to push her out of the picture plane into our space. This was never intended to be a portrait of anyone specific – we know this because she wears exotic dress not worn in seventeenth-century Holland – but a more timeless figure from history. A tiny speck in the right corner of her mouth indicates she has just licked her lips, and her mouth is open as if she is speaking. But she keeps silent, and has a mysterious air that never fails to intrigue. In effect, Vermeer has left it to us to fill in her thoughts.

Jean-Baptiste-Siméon Chardin
Paris 1699–1799 Paris

Still Life with a Copper Pot, Cheese and Eggs, c.1730–5

Oil on canvas, 33 × 41 cm

Bequest of Abraham Bredius, 1946

MH 656

This last painting is an odd duck in the collection. Neither Dutch nor Flemish, it is by the French artist Chardin. Former director Abraham Bredius bought it in 1901 at an auction in London and lent it immediately to the Mauritshuis. When he died in 1946 Bredius left this work and twenty-five others to the museum, many of which are important works that are always on display. Some have claimed that this still life is an anomaly in the Mauritshuis, and should be given or lent to another museum. Bredius stipulated in his will that all of the paintings he left to the Mauritshuis must always remain there and may never be lent out to another institution. There is a very good case to be made for keeping this Chardin in the collection. In the first place, it is a masterpiece by one of the greatest still-life painters, whose work is characterised by subtle plays of light and colour. The picture also betrays the influence of Dutch and Flemish art, and it can be compared to several works in the collection of the Mauritshuis. The composition, with its table ledge, reminds us of Coorte. The humble subject matter is very close to Clara Peeters' painting. The detailed rendering of the objects harks back to Dutch genre paintings. The play of light evokes the great master Vermeer. This still life will remain on display in the Mauritshuis as a reminder of the continuing influence of Dutch and Flemish painting on the generations of artists who have followed.

First published in 2014 by
Scala Arts & Heritage Publishers Ltd
10 Lion Yard, Tremadoc Road
London SW4 7NQ, UK
Tel: +44 (0) 20 7808 1550
www.scalapublishers.com

In association with
Royal Picture Gallery Mauritshuis
Plein 29
2511 CS The Hague
Netherlands
Tel. +31 70 302 3456
www.mauritshuis.nl

ISBN 978-1-85759-847-6

Edited by Esme West
Designed by Nigel Soper
Printed in Turkey

10 9 8 7 6 5 4 3 2

FRONT COVER:
Detail of ***Girl with a Pearl Earring***
by Johannes Vermeer (see pp.76–7)

BACK COVER:
Detail of ***The Garden of Eden with the Fall of Man***
by Jan Brueghel the Elder and Peter Paul Rubens
(see pp.12–13)

FRONTISPIECE:
Detail of ***View of Delft***
by Johannes Vermeer (see pp.74–5)